Poetry M

Hereford & Worcestershire
Edited by Chris Hallam

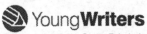 Young**Writers**

First published in Great Britain in 2004 by:
Young Writers
Remus House
Coltsfoot Drive
Peterborough
PE2 9JX
Telephone: 01733 890066
Website: www.youngwriters.co.uk

SB ISBN 1 84460 415 2

Foreword

This year, the Young Writers' 'Poetry In Motion' competition proudly presents a showcase of the best poetic talent selected from over 40,000 up-and-coming writers nationwide.

Young Writers was established in 1991 to promote the reading and writing of poetry within schools and to the youth of today. Our books nurture and inspire confidence in the ability of young writers and provide a snapshot of poems written in schools and at home by budding poets of the future.

The thought effort, imagination and hard work put into each poem impressed us all and the task of selecting poems was a difficult but nevertheless enjoyable experience.

We hope you are as pleased as we are with the final selection and that you and your family continue to be entertained with *Poetry In Motion Hereford & Worcestershire* for many years to come.

Contents

Jessica Cummins (12)	71
Matthew Buckley (13)	72
Faye Stanley (12)	73
Abbey Brett (13)	74
Daniel Hemming (12)	75
Tom Melbourne (12)	76
Phil Southall (13)	77
Emily Claydon (12)	78
Laura Baxter (12)	79
Daniel Crane (13)	80
Casey Nokes (13)	81
Emma Broom (12)	82
Kelly Davitt (12)	83
Amy Youster (12)	84
Laura Halfpenny (13)	85
Sophie Hazell (12)	86
Kate Walters (12)	87
Owen Long (12)	88
Sam Morris (12)	89
Danielle Hill (12)	90
Sophie Tilley (13)	91
Lucy Howard (12)	92

St Bede's Catholic Middle School, Redditch

Hannah Walker (12)	93
Katy McCullagh (11)	94
Amber O'Shaughnessy (12)	95
James Murphy (11)	96
Natasha Daplyn (13)	97
James Down (11)	98
Grace Taylor & Maria Hore (11)	99
James Brandon (12)	100
Lauren O'Brien (12)	101
David Phelan (12)	102
Annabell McAuliffe (12)	103
Laura Cunning (11)	104
Jordan-Leigh Norman (12)	105
Christy Connolly (12)	106
Stephanie Taylor	107
Rachel White (12)	108
Fahren Lee (12)	109

The Poems

The Sun

The sun is in my eyes
The sun is in my head
The sun is in the sky
When I'm upset I still see the sun
I'm kind and helpful I see the sun
I'll always see the sun

Bright yellow sun
Nearly blinding me
Cover up the sun, clouds please, please, please
So I'll see again.

Eloise Gibb (11)
Bishop Perowne CE High School, Worcester

All Alone

I talk to myself
I think to myself
It seems I walk down a slope by myself
I seek the end of a tunnel by myself
I tread through the mist by myself
I am all alone by myself
I am sacrificed alone by myself
Vanished from all human beings
Beyond nature
Alone.

Ryan Biggerstaff (11)
Bishop Perowne CE High School, Worcester

Post Mort

I never wanted to go in,
I wish I'd never been dared by him,
If I could turn back the hands of time,
I wouldn't have to say this rhyme.

As I went slowly to the gates,
I turned and saw his grinning face,
I opened up the iron doors,
Went in and saw the cracked floorboards.

I saw a door and turned the keys,
And it opened with great ease,
I was scared and I knew it,
But the door was now open so I went through it.

There were pictures on the walls,
Of babies, toys and bouncing balls,
Very odd in a place like this?
Then I saw something I couldn't miss.

There was a figure standing tall,
I couldn't see him, the light was too small,
He started walking up to me,
Then his face, that I could see.

His eyes were red, a deep, deep red,
That moment, I wished that I was dead,
But soon he made my wish come true,
He cut off my head, he cut me in two.

I sometimes walk up and down the roads,
I follow people, but nobody knows,
Sometimes, I remember the cries,
Believe me, for I tell no lies.

Liz Crawford (12)
Bishop Perowne CE High School, Worcester

Which Is Witch?

'Hee! Hee! Hee!'
Cackled the witches times three,
'Children taste best,
When cooked with lemon zest,
To get some, we have to find a fool,
I know, let's go to school!'

The witch with the warty nose,
Put on tatty children's clothes,
The witch with the large bum,
Started to chew gum,
The last witch, scariest of all three,
Stirred the cauldron with the branch of a tree!

'Cats, bats and centipedes,
Start this spell to grant our needs,
To find a fool and make him groan,
We need to explore *Bishop Perowne!*

When we have him in our power,
We have to make him sweet not sour,
Then we'll wrench him limb from limb,
And suck the flesh right off him,
The bones will go into a soup
And cooked inside a large tureen,
Then we'll charge 50p
And sell it in the canteen!

Little will they know,
That they'll all be eating little Joe!

So kids welcome us, when you see us at the gate,
But by then, it will be . . .
Too late!'

Kelly Stinton (12)
Bishop Perowne CE High School, Worcester

Hallowe'en

I opened up the creaky door,
There I saw upon the floor,
A jet-black bat fallen from flight,
On this spooky Hallowe'en night.

I walked along the misty streets,
The children playing trick or treats,
As the moon was nearly full,
I saw a shape of a ghostly skull.

It rose and circled above my head,
The eyes inside were ruby red,
A clap of thunder,
Made me wonder,

Why am I out here,
In terrible fear?
I saw a vampire sucking blood,
He dropped the body, it made a thud.

I screamed, I knew I had to run,
I needn't fear, because here's the sun.

Olivia Harris (12)
Bishop Perowne CE High School, Worcester

Horror Poem

One eerie night when the rain pelted down,
There I stood my face in a frown.
My heart was beating so very, very fast,
Was it a dream? How long will it last?

The hairs on my back were standing on edge,
Then I saw some rustling over by that hedge.
I started to panic, what a scary life,
When all of a sudden came a man with a knife!
I ran and ran till I could hardly breathe,
Was this real or make-believe?
I ran until I couldn't see the man anymore,
Then I stopped still, my feet rooted to the floor.
I still couldn't see it was really very hard,
But I knew where I was I was in a graveyard.
I looked down upon a stone,
The name that was written was my very own!
The man that was following me came into sight,
The long silver blade glistening in the moonlight.
I stumbled back hitting a tree,
Then all I felt was the knife entering me!
I heard the man scream more and more,
As he watched my guts spill onto the floor.
Then all I remember is hitting the ground,
I couldn't see anything or hear any sound!

Jody Hudspith (12)
Bishop Perowne CE High School, Worcester

Vampire Castle

As I walk through the castle gate
I hear lightning behind me
I pull up my hood
And walk faster.
As I walk through the halls
All is quiet
Except a whisper
And the howls of the wolves
As I walk up the stairs
The pictures seem to move
And I tremble
As the walls seem to slowly close in.
As I walk along the corridor
To the room at the end
I feel cold and clammy
As the screams slowly get louder.
As I stand outside the room
I pull out the stake
And the cross
getting ready.
As I kick open the door
The woman lies dead
And the vampire
Leans over her.
As I show him the cross
He cowers in fear
The wind blows open the window.
As the thunder roars loud
I push in the stake
And the vampire is no more.

Jack Gilliard (12)
Bishop Perowne CE High School, Worcester

The Greedy Alligator

I have a rather greedy pet,
A little alligator,
When he my younger sister met,
He opened wide and ate her.

But soon he learned that he
Was wrong,
To eat the child in question,
For he felt bad before too long
And suffered indigestion.

This story seems to prove to me,
That he who rudely gobbles,
Will soon regret his gluttony
And get the collywobbles!

Vicky Cook (12)
Bishop Perowne CE High School, Worcester

Where's The Bell?

Ding-dong! Ding-dong!
Phew, there goes the bell
Lessons are too long
It's lunchtime at last

Games are played
Shoes are scuffed
Squabbles are made
Lunch is eaten

Teachers sit in the staffroom, cosy as can be
We are freezing cold
They are drinking tea!
Hurry up, bell! Hurry up, bell!

Naomi Brooker (11)
Bishop Perowne CE High School, Worcester

My First Day At High School

It's time to start my new high school,
I feel very worried cos I am quite small.
In the playground kids rushing to and fro,
We are all not sure where we have to go.

Then the tutors came out and called our names
And shouted, 'Come along children that's the end of games!
Please line up and follow me,
I'll show you all where you're all meant to be.'

We all followed quietly to our tutor rooms,
Ms Devereaux said, 'We're in room P22.'
So we all sat and waited for our student planner
And filled them in a sensible manner.

Before I knew it the day had ended,
My first day at Bishop's I'd say was splendid.

Louisa Tyrrell (11)
Bishop Perowne CE High School, Worcester

Homework

When teachers give homework
All the class moan and groan,
The teacher tells them all off
And they get sent right home.

When teachers give out homework
All the mums and dads groan and moan,
They complain that they don't get it,
Then the teacher calls people on the phone.

When children give out homework
All the teachers moan and groan,
The children tell them all off
And they get sent right home.

Olivia Knight (11)
Bishop Perowne CE High School, Worcester

Shadows Of Death!

Walking through the alley of death,
Where many people let out their last breath.
Superstitions and secrets lurk in the shadows,
Like cats and mice in meadows.
Shuffling and scuttling, sighing and swaying,
The sounds delaying the safe warmth of home.
How different it looks in the warm midday sun.
No skeleton prodding you on with a gun!
A snap from behind brought me to life to see,
The shadow of a man with a knife.
The jagged edges piercing the sharp,
The silhouette flew out from the dark,
Creeping up from behind.
The victim wheeled round eager to see
The night's hungry clown.
The knife sank in further and screams from him fled,
Like maggots and worms unto the dead.
Pushing the knife in like corkscrew and cork.
The night and dark made everything good,
The crime scene, the murder, understood.
The shadows of death had risen again,
Take me with them like eagles and then
Soaring and soaring away from the crime,
They took and they took till eventually . . .
I died!

Becky Taylor (12)
Bishop Perowne CE High School, Worcester

Why?

Why is poetry important?
That's all I want to know
It's funny and effective
And it's not boring and slow.

Why is poetry important?
Tell me please oh do
It can be about anything you like
Even your smelly shoe.

Why is poetry important?
Is it there to tell a story?
Pretty sweet and nice
Or blood, guts or something gory.

Why is poetry important?
I think I understand
It can be on this planet
Or on another land.

Amanda Bent (11)
Bishop Perowne CE High School, Worcester

The Night Before Christmas

The white night came,
So exciting no fear,
Shining bright lights,
Christmas is here!

Door to door,
Santa would go,
Reindeer dancing,
Through the crisp snow!

Children asleep,
No sound, so still,
Stockings hung high,
Above the window sill!

Down he came,
Through the sooty hole,
Twisting and turning,
As he sat on the coal!

As he crept,
Along the floorboards,
Eating and slurping,
In his long trouser cords!

Dropping in presents,
As he walked,
Tiptoeing quietly,
Never talked!

Off he went,
Sack in hand,
Up the chimney,
Through the sand!

Ready and waiting,
Then suddenly gone,
Children awoke,
As the sun shone!

Kelly Stinton & Kathleen Thomson (12)
Bishop Perowne CE High School, Worcester

Fifty-Six Croxley Street

Fifty-six Croxley Street
Is where the ghosts like to meet

I creep past on my way home,
In the dead of night
I'm all alone.

All boarded up, windows blind
Thoughts spinning in my mind

I'm drawn to the house, though it is late
I enter the garden through the creaking gate

My footsteps ring hollowly on the path
I think I hear a distant laugh

In the garden I can see
Shapes and shadows that mimic me

Peering through the keyhole crack
Peeling paint, dusty and black

Face so white
It lights up the dark of night

Running, running through the night,
Running hard with all my might!

George Devereux (12)
Bishop Perowne CE High School, Worcester

The Panther

Panther, panther as black as night,
Looking for a fearsome fight,
Prowling round looking for prey,
Prowling round waiting for day.

When day comes he goes for cover,
Whilst the rest of his family look for one another,
It's easier at night he can't be seen,
That's when he can live on the line, be extreme.

Finally his wait is over; he spots a bird,
He stops dead still so he can't be heard,
He pounces towards it, but it flies away,
I guess he will have to wait for another day.

Rowena Davis (13)
Bishop Perowne CE High School, Worcester

Playtime

All the people on the playground
Happy, dancing, singing and screaming
Happy laughs and unhappy cries
Some people sometimes dreaming lies
All the dinner ladies with their walkie-talkies
Always remember naughty talking
On the playground there's people having fun
Until the bell rings out comes the walking, talking nun
While some people are walking in
Others are kicking empty tins
On the playground you have so much fun
But next there's lunch fun, fun, fun.

James Acheson-Hill (11)
Bishop Perowne CE High School, Worcester

I Want To Be A Teacher

I want to be a teacher
When I am all grown up.
I'll sit in the school staffroom
And drink tea by the cup,
I'll give the kids a hard time
They'll stay in from play,
Forced to watch the other kids
Having fun all day.

They will all give me presents
Of candles and of wines.
I will drink the booze all day
Not walking in straight lines.
Teachers don't do anything
Just drink cups of tea;
I will do whatever I want
Happy as can be.

I want to be a teacher
I'll make boring, funny!
I'll watch the rest suffer
And still get the money!
And guess what I will spend it on?
Bags of PG Tips
So I can drink loads more tea
Eating jelly cherry lips.

Morwenna Francis (11)
Bishop Perowne CE High School, Worcester

Terrible Teachers

I ran through the changing room,
Relieved to get away,
The horrid teacher, the things he said!
He brought me to dismay,
A point is certain for talking,
Maybe a detention too,
This simply terrible teacher,
May even pick on you.
His smelly breath is revolting,
It expands through the room
And his loud treacherous voice,
Goes, *boom, boom, boom,*
Their looks are worse than our garden features,
Horrible, nasty, *terrible teachers.*

Michael Shipley (11)
Bishop Perowne CE High School, Worcester

School Report

Could do better
> isn't bothered
>> doesn't even try

disrupts the class
> is always last
>> makes other children cry.

What have you got
> to say for yourself?
>> You're bad.

You're mad
> and you're rude.

Wow! Thanks Mum
> that's brilliant
>> I told you I'd improve.

Joe Collins (11)
Bishop Perowne CE High School, Worcester

My Home Poem

Home is simply a place to eat
and run and jump and sleep.
Home is a place full of stuff,
but sometimes with big brothers
it's a bit too rough.
You can watch television in style
and watch Linford Christie run a mile.
You can have pets in your house
you can even keep a mouse.
Read a book or try and cook
but to me home is a safe place
and somewhere to invite my mates.

Nicole Booth (13)
Bishop Perowne CE High School, Worcester

Peace . . . Peace . . . Peace!

There's never any quiet.
I'm sitting doing my homework.
3 8s are . . .
'Hannah, where's the rubber?'
'I don't know.'
3 8s are 24 aren't they? I'm not sure.
'Hannah, can you take this upstairs please?'
'Later!'
I'm frustrated now. It's harder to concentrate.
What are 3 8s, come on, I do know.
'Waaahh!'
Oh no, they're at it again.
'He hit me!'
'But he was annoying me!'
I want some quiet.
'Can you two stop it please?'
Back to 3 8s. I'm sure they're 24. Aren't I?
'Hannah, why is your room such a mess?'
'It's how I like it!'
'Hannah, where have you put my book?'
'Hannah, where . . . ?'
Hannah this, Hannah that. I'm mad.
I want them to stop. There's never any peace.
'Can you lot give me some peace!'
At least they're quiet now. 3 8s are 24.
Let's move on.
'Hannah, where's that new game?'
'Argh!'

Hannah Sansome (11)
Bishop Perowne CE High School, Worcester

I Wish My Name Wasn't Claire . . .

Claire, clean your bedroom.
Claire, help with the washing up.
I wish my name wasn't Claire.
Claire, clean your school shoes.
Claire, do your homework.
I wish my name wasn't Claire.
Claire, clean your teeth.
Claire, do your school bag.
I wish my name wasn't Claire.
Claire, go to bed.
Claire, go and have a bath.
I wish my name wasn't Claire.
Claire, we love you!
I'm glad my name is Claire.

Claire Nottingham (12)
Bishop Perowne CE High School, Worcester

My Home Poem

My home is nice,
Nice and light,
That's why I am so tight.

My walls are big,
Pouring with light,
It feels like I am in Heaven.

I like my bed,
So comfy and soft,
That's why I'm always tired,

I like my Xbox,
It's full of fun,
That's when my life had just begun.

Martin Jelfs (13)
Bishop Perowne CE High School, Worcester

Home Sweet Home

I like my home, my home is fun,
My home is somewhere where I'm on the run.
I wouldn't swap my home, for anything in the world,
Even if my home were rubbish and it swayed and swirled.
My home is great it has all my daily needs,
There's stuff all over the place for every deed.
I love my home, my home is ace,
It surely is the bestest place.

Josh Turvey (13)
Bishop Perowne CE High School, Worcester

My Home

M y family lives in together in my home
Y ou might think it is just a building

H aving a lovely environment is a home
O ur home is always a safe place to be
M any people today are without homes
E verybody should have a home
no matter who they are.

Jennifer Young (13)
Bishop Perowne CE High School, Worcester

My Home

My home is a place where I like to be,
Full of nice things especially my family.
There is love, there is support.
My home is safe, my home is warm,
To keep me sheltered from the storm.

I have a lovely bedroom,
Which is full of things I adore.
I am a lucky girl who couldn't ask for more.
My bedroom is cosy, my bedroom is bright
I could stay there all day and all night.

In my bedroom I have a nice bed,
It's warm, soft and cosy and comfy for my head.
My pillow is fluffy and my quilt is big and puffy.

And altogether my house is warm, cosy, bright and secure
And a place of happiness which I adore.

Kirsty Gardner (13)
Bishop Perowne CE High School, Worcester

My Home

My home means to me
A nice warm place
And security

My home includes
My mum
My dad
My brother
me
Plus my dog, Shankly

I love my home
It means everything to me
I don't think I want to ever leave.

Lucy Williams (12)
Bishop Perowne CE High School, Worcester

Home

Home is where the heart is,
It's got everything I need,
It's got
My mum
My dad
My younger sister
And most importantly, me.

It's where
I do my homework
And sit and watch TV
It's where I sit and write songs for my band
And am happy being me.

Samantha Blight (13)
Bishop Perowne CE High School, Worcester

What Home Means To Me

What my home means to me,
a safe place to go with security,
unconditional love, something to eat,
a place to relax with a cup of tea
and the little darlings, you know the pets
it's not always perfect all the time
but it is better than nothing, right.

Joshua Hicks (13)
Bishop Perowne CE High School, Worcester

Seasons

It's November now and autumn is here,
dark nights, warm fires, it's that time of year!
Gathering up all the fallen leaves,
looking around at the empty trees.

Now it's December and the cold is here,
autumn's gone and winter's near.
This is the time for scarves and gloves
and cuddling up to the ones you love!

The daffodils are rising, the lambs are being born,
spring has arrived and the fields are full of corn.
The bluebells are in the meadow, the grass is long and green,
the birds are singing sweetly and the air is clear and clean!

The sun is hot and shining bright,
be careful that the bees don't bite.
Summer's here so put on your hat,
I can't think of any more so that's that!

Kelly Nicholls (13)
Bishop Perowne CE High School, Worcester

My Home

Home sweet home
Is where love is found
Happiness has frowned
In that home of mine
Where the care is spread
Like butter on a piece of bread
The love you can feel
Does not peel
It simply stays forever
Home sweet home
Is where the love is found
Happiness is brought
Nobody has frowned.

Vicky Pomeroy (13)
Bishop Perowne CE High School, Worcester

My Magic Box

(Based on 'Magic Box' by Kit Wright)

I will put in the box
The silent glint of a dangling icicle,
The creamy glow of the stars I see each night.
The swift movement of a rampaging Chinese dragon.

I will put in the box
The bright yellowy colour of the sun each morning,
The first laugh of a newborn baby,
The melt of butter on your tongue.

I will put in the box
The longest necklace ever made from bold pearls and mini rubies,
The snowflakes on a frosty morning landing on my hand,
A pair of pixie's wings, the softest in the land.

I will put in the box
The world's funniest joke told by my mum in the only way she can,
The smell of a fresh bun with cinnamon in the corners,
The clink of coins jangled together in a copper dish.

My box is fashioned from
The scales of the last crispy white dragon,
With my name engraved in the corners
And a sun and cloud skilfully painted on top.

I gently stroll on my box
Calmly in the soft breeze,
The fresh smell of cut grass
And enjoy the scarlet sky.

Alex Perry (12)
Blackminster Middle School, Evesham

Surfing

Just you and your board and the ocean blue
The wide open sea comes to welcome you
Waves crash like thunder over your head
Without a swift mind you're better off dead
You fly like a bullet shot from a gun,
Then hold your head high and surf to the sun.

David Horton (11)
Blackminster Middle School, Evesham

Imagination

Do you get told to use your
    Imagination?
I use mine when someone's a bore
    You see,

I can climb any mountain,
Fly past any star,
Make a sculpture fountain,
Or even land on Mars!

I know,
Anything can be achieved with,
    Imagination.

On a regular basis,
I travel to Venice,
But today I found the case is:
I am inside Greece!

I know,
Anything can be achieved with,
    Imagination.

I can travel all over the world,
While still in my bed,
When I am meant to be working:
I'm adventuring instead!

I adventure,
With only imagination for company.

Emily Moore (11)
Blackminster Middle School, Evesham

The Mystery Girl

She longed to be a bird
So that she could fly away
But it seemed that wish could never come true
And so there she lay

Some said she wished too hard
Some said she wished too long
But one day when they awoke
They found that she was gone

The trees they said stood witness
The sky refused to tell
She pitied every blade of grass
She was captured in a spell

She spread her arms out wide
And at the crack of dawn
She let go of everything
And then she was gone.

Stephanie Spiers (12)
Blackminster Middle School, Evesham

Ten Things Found In A Zookeeper's Pocket

A bag of food,
An old souvenir
And a key for an old trapdoor.
A dictionary of animals,
A red, purple and blue pen
And a stuffed elephant that comes to life.
A dog's collar,
A photo of a monkey
And a pair of eyes for the back of his head.
What a strange pocketful!

Sarah-Jane Keen (12)
Blackminster Middle School, Evesham

Henry

Henry is an unwanted baby
He is like a pile of frogspawn
Left to live and work for himself
Henry is a nimble chimney brush
With no life or feeling

He sounds like silence
As nobody even listens to him
He wears sooty rags
And is full of untreated wounds
He hasn't any face or hair
Just a sooty mess
Placed upon his shoulders.

Phil Jones (12)
Blackminster Middle School, Evesham

Enjoy Sports

I love to run, to hop and to skip
Having fun not needing a kip
I want to do these for the rest of my life,
When I'm a teen and when I'm old
You only live once
Do all the sports you can
Winning and losing is just part of the plan!

Christie Judge (11)
Blackminster Middle School, Evesham

Autumn Times

Autumn is a time of year
Where animals hibernate far and near
Birds fly east and west
Humans put on vests.

Fire burn, burn, burn, burn
Earth turn, turn, turn, turn.

Animals sleep, dogs weep
The leaves change
Animals' behaviour a different range.

Fire burn, burn, burn, burn
Earth turn, turn, turn, turn.

The leaves red, brown and gold
Autumn weather is very cold.
The people play
Every day.

Fire burn, burn, burn, burn
Earth turn, turn, turn, turn.

Heather Pettifer (12)
Blackminster Middle School, Evesham

Rocking, Rolling On The Stairs

Rocking, rolling on the stairs,
My brother watches me and stares.
'What are you doing?' he asks me.
'What do you think?
Rocking, rolling on the stairs.'

Francesca Pratt (11)
Blackminster Middle School, Evesham

Lo

Dissipate my heart's desires
To save them from Lolita's mires.
Be gone; be banished far away,
For here they cannot sanely stay
In company of thoughts who flail
And swallow up the banshee's wail.

A miser hoarding caitiffs wild
Will note ambitions I have piled
As vagrants coined of rain and storm;
Born frozen; children never warm;
Poor rigid souls dragged over pyres
That now construct my makeshift fires.

Yet I refrain to strike the match
And long await dead hopes to hatch
Compiling showcase, one on one,
To clamber onto each born numb.

As violation makes insane
And mutes these gentle dreams in brain
A channel drills from Humbert's mind
Distorting acid left behind
To rally round like fleas on ice
Who slip and slide into their heist

And long remain whilst he cannot
To further fester in his rot
Until the muzzle barks the shot
That duly barrels out my lot.

O heart, divide this love of foe,
My symbiotic pact with woe
Act just to leave in devastation
Bounty pure for recreation.

Rachel Sykes (17)
Hereford Sixth Form College, Hereford

Black Lights

Crying acid tears,
they melt my skin,
make me bleed
and I think of you
looking at the glass.
Staring at these transparent scars,
tracing them with uncaring hands,
your name, over and over.

The glass,
now broken from staring too long,
cuts my hands, making tiny holes.
I connect the dots.
Your name, over and over,
Yet I don't recognise the letters.

They form like constellations,
then trickle down my arms.
Nothing more than a bloody mess,
burnt-out stars.
Sedated perfection,
hidden truths,
terrifying yet beautiful.
As my eyes apologise for their sins.

Looking across the width of the night,
I can see you breathing in the toxic dawn.
Let me sleep a little while longer. Please.
I take comfort in the darkness,
In knowing I'll never be seen.
I'm never seen in daylight either,
But the light makes it hurt.
The darkness conceals all wounds . . .
All people.

Bryony Edwards (17)
Newent Community School, Newent

The Revenge

Hitler and his men were surrounded,
While the Russians pounded.
In the meantime, the Americans, they were grounded
On the banks of hell in Normandy.
But Hitler still fought for death and glory
But he still would have no sparkling glory.

Stephen Boyle (12)
Parkside Middle School, Bromsgrove

Blusha

Blusha's in da house,
Me na run like a mouse,
Mouse!
He na run like a mouse from your house.
From your lyrical flow,
You may have da doe,
But I have da flow,
I don't have time for your pants rhyme
Your rhymes are pants,
With your colony of ants.

Ella Ralph (12)
Parkside Middle School, Bromsgrove

A Jet, A Car, A Train

A jet flying in the sky,
Zooming past the birds.
A jet flying in the sky,
Zooming past the kites that people fly.

A car riding down the road,
Speeding past the people on the path.
A car riding down the road,
Speeding past the animals and trees.

A train skimming on the track,
Speeding past the people that are waiting.
A train skimming on the track
Speeding past the animals in the countryside.

A jet, a car, a train.
All speeding by.
Without a seat belt, if you crash,
You will die.

Stephen Brighton (12)
Parkside Middle School, Bromsgrove

My Journey

I am going in the car,
to the Hawthorns
It isn't far.

On the motorway I go,
speeding fast
not going slow.

Out the window
I can see
lots of fields passing me.

Stopping, stopping,
I can see
the car park space is near me.

I am walking down the street
into the stadium
I find my seat.

I have had a
football thrill
West Brom beat Portsmouth 5-0.

Andrew McDiarmid (12)
Parkside Middle School, Bromsgrove

A Horse's Day

Horses eat grass
as they pass.
They have a brush
as they blush.
They are cute
as they play the flute.
They like mints
and treats like sweets.
Some horses are tall,
some are small.
Some are fat,
some are thin.
Stables they sleep in,
people sweep in.
Horses run in the wind,
they play with the others.
Horses run and jump a lot.

Lydia Whitehouse (12)
Parkside Middle School, Bromsgrove

Castle

Castle, castle
cold and dark.
Castle, castle
monsters will lark.

Castle, castle
you must beware.
Castle, castle
you are in for a scare.

Castle, castle
compared to the thug.
Castle, castle
you are like a bug.

Michael Owen (12)
Parkside Middle School, Bromsgrove

Water

Trickling down a stream like a snake over sand.
Water can be your lifeline or could be your killer.
When it touches your lips, it can taste so sweet.
Water can be fun but can be dangerous.
You use it for cooking and other lessons
So then water is lovely, liquid water.

Kiefer Hanman (12)
Parkside Middle School, Bromsgrove

The Black Car

Car in the day,
Car at night
Speeding past
As fast as light.

The colour is black,
As black as the night.
Nowhere near
As bright as light.

Racing all night
Up and down
Best driver wins a crown
Racing until it is light.

Andy Lowe (13)
Parkside Middle School, Bromsgrove

All The Seasons

Summer is hot and weary
Summer is nice and dreamy
And summer is nice and hot
Summer means we can go in the swimming pool

Autumn, the weather is cold
Autumn, the leaves are falling off the trees
And autumn, there's no swimming pools out.

Winter means loads of presents
Winter means loads of snow
And winter means snowmen.

Jodie Butt (12)
Parkside Middle School, Bromsgrove

Summer's End

Winter is coming,
Summer's end is near.
The leaves are falling,
Coats are here.
The summer sun
Is at the end
Christmas presents and trees
Are around the bend.
People's short shorts
And T-shirts are at an end.
The snow is here,
Bye-bye summer come back
When winter's end is near!

Ollie Hartshorne (12)
Parkside Middle School, Bromsgrove

In English

In English
I can't rhyme
But I can whine.
I said, 'Miss
I can't rhyme
But I can whine.
Why Miss?'
Like I said
I can't rhyme
But I can whine.

Emily Elizabeth Field (12)
Parkside Middle School, Bromsgrove

My Dog

He is black
and he lives in a sack
and he hits beehives
and slobber dribbles out of his mouth
and his health is bad.

He eats food out of his bowl.
Sometimes he gets in a mood
and he is a cool dude.

Adam Boroughs (12)
Parkside Middle School, Bromsgrove

Maths

Tick-tock, tick-tock
The clock's tick, when will it end?
Maths lesson,
Last session.
On a Friday afternoon
9 times 7, 8 times 3.
I need some help
Hear my plea.

Square root, cubed and squared
This lesson gets me really scared.
1 add 2, 2 add 3
Now hear my plea.
I can't do this, I'm no good,
Just when will this lesson end?

Natalie Clifford (12)
Parkside Middle School, Bromsgrove

War

It crawls along
The midnight moon
To listen to
The dooming soon.

It seems to watch
The timing clock
But soon it will
Reach the top.

Then as it goes
Along the floor,
It turns into
A body's core

And everywhere
There's blood and bones
To rot away
Beneath the stones.

Rosie Frost (12)
Parkside Middle School, Bromsgrove

Colours

Blue is like a shivering stream,
White is a lovely dream,
Silver is the rattle of chains,
Yellow is laughter,
Gold is a trumpet call,
Orange is luminous flames,
Grey is a misty sky,
Red is a scream, a strangled cry,
Black is a gunshot, the end of your life.

Rosie-May Baylis-Wright (12)
Parkside Middle School, Bromsgrove

The Enchanted Forest

I walked past the tall green trees,
Across the bridge.
I began to feel the cool breeze,
The clear blue water beneath me.

The bright coloured flowers shelter land,
As I follow the pebbly path.
I stop and stand
As the pond grows nearer.

I can now hear the trickling water,
The drooping trees hang near.
I can see the lily pads,
But nothing can I hear.

The delightful feeling,
There's no time to wait.
The sun's getting low,
I can't be late.

Lisa Davis (13)
Parkside Middle School, Bromsgrove

Splashy Seaside

As I hear the pebbles crash,
I see the water going splash.
As I sit upon the sand,
I see a couple clenching hands.

As I see children in the sea,
It feels like it should be me.
It is getting very late now
Where has the day gone, I wonder how.

Kellie-Jade Steer (12)
Parkside Middle School, Bromsgrove

The Seaside

I sit upon the sand so quiet
First I hear the waves go bang
Against the sharp rocks they go clang.

I here the giggles of young children
I then hear the splash of the sea
From where they paddle toe to knee.

Chelsie Lewis (12)
Parkside Middle School, Bromsgrove

Bird

Look up in the sky,
What do you see?
Do you see clouds
Or do you see me?

For I am a bird
Flying through the sky.
Don't know where I'm going
And I don't know why.

Jack Chorley (12)
Parkside Middle School, Bromsgrove

World War II

Blood has been shed,
There's lots to be said.
People to be found
Or buried under the ground.

Oh God let them fly,
Those ones that did die.
Think what they did give,
Just to let us live.

Those wives that cried,
For their husbands that died.
Those husbands that returned
Stopped their wives from being concerned.

Stuart Parsons (12)
Parkside Middle School, Bromsgrove

Poetry

Poetry, poetry,
always rhymes.
Poetry, poetry,
appears all the time.

Poetry, poetry,
different shapes and sizes.
Poetry, poetry,
lots of small surprises.

Poetry, poetry,
long or short lines.
Poetry, poetry,
fun all the time.

Poetry, poetry,
Goes on forever.
Poetry, poetry,
To be read in any weather.

Poetry, poetry,
it's in a book.
Poetry, poetry,
come and have a look.

Poetry, poetry,
like it or lump it.
Poetry, poetry,
do what you see fit.

Poetry, poetry,
who wrote it first?
Poetry, poetry,
this is poetic outburst.

Ben Turnbull (12)
Parkside Middle School, Bromsgrove

Dog Doorbell

How will we know
That's the question?
With the dog bark, bark, barking,
How will we ever know?

With annoying habits,
Scratching at the door,
Loosening the paintwork
Then we'll get angry.

Let's help poor little dogs,
Let's have an idea.
Let's make something for them,
Perhaps a dog doorbell.

With a panel each side of the door,
Connected to the doorbell.
Each time he scratches
You'll hear the doorbell ring-ring-ringing.

Will it work
Or will it fail.
Let's wait and see,
Let's give it a try.

But what will happen,
When the dog sharpens his claws.
Not wanting to go outside.
We'll soon get fed up of the doorbell ringing.

Louise Dawes (12)
Parkside Middle School, Bromsgrove

Hamster

Hamster! Hamster! standing there
In the dark very aware,
Of the noises in the night
That would give one such a fright.

In the cage the hamster dude
Gathers up all her food.
For the hunger of the day
When she does not come out to play.

As she plays she feels a lump
And knows that it must be a dump.
Then she starts to push and push
And out comes a big pile of mush.

When the sun begins to rise
The warm mush attracts the flies.
She curls up and goes to sleep
In a warm and cosy heap.

Emily Harper (12)
Parkside Middle School, Bromsgrove

A New Start

My heart is beating very fast,
As I think about all my past.
The things that happened, the things I did
As I thought back to when I was a kid.

The shame, the sorrow, the hurt, the pain,
As I try to stop thinking, it happens again.
I look up to the sky, it seems so still
As my tears shed, there is no thrill.

Everything seems to have disappeared
All this is just what I had feared.
I dread each moment as it goes by,
All I want to do is sit and cry.

Everything seems to revolve around sadness
But I just wish it revolved around gladness.
What am I to do, there's nothing to live for
I feel so weak, life seems such a bore.

So maybe I'll get up and live life to the full,
Life's too short to sit and be dull.
So I'll stop thinking about the past and think of the future,
It could be hard to forget, so I'll try my very best.

I've already wasted life, so I'll settle down,
There's gonna be a new me, I won't let myself down.
I'm gonna give myself courage and aim high,
Just say to myself, 'I can do it!' and look up to the sky.

Maria Bishton (12)
Parkside Middle School, Bromsgrove

The Ghostly Galleon

The wind swept the gushing sea,
As the thunderclouds covered the crystal moon.
The waves surfed rapidly over the mass of the icy skin of the water,
As the mist spread rapidly over the mass of the ocean.

In the far distance a wave so light and so small crossed the ocean,
The mist parted whilst a ghostly galleon crawled from the unknown.

In a chamber far aloft, a cry of the once forgotten,
A dying victim, uttered sounds in an echo,
The creaking on the stubbly wood sounds.

The tattered flags that with the frozen wind
Seemed like the old wave of lost memory.
The ghost of the galleon sailed swiftly to seek its tale of murder.

Rebecca Parker (13)
Parkside Middle School, Bromsgrove

Bonfire Night

Boom and crackle all night long,
Fireworks shooting with lovely colours
Some blue, yellow, red even purple
Sometimes sparkle in the sky.
Fairgrounds all lit up
With people screaming, even jumping
When the fireworks go off with a *bang!*

Zennah Wakefield (12)
Parkside Middle School, Bromsgrove

The Lake District

When I'm walking down a stony lane
Or when I'm climbing high,
I see the trees in the forest,
I hear the lambs bleating in the field,
I feel the cold air on my face,
I taste the fresh rain,
And I smell hot coal on the fire.
This is my favourite place.

Genny Billington (12)
Parkside Middle School, Bromsgrove

Winter Land

Winter, winter is coming,
Christmas bells are drumming
Night so dark
Stroll in the park.
Winter, winter is coming.

Twinkle, twinkle light,
Stars are shining bright.
Snowy grounds,
Silent sounds,
Twinkle, twinkle light.

Wrapping, wrapping gifts,
Never time to sit.
Frosty nights,
Smile with delight,
Wrapping, wrapping gifts.

Money, money spent,
Christmas pressies sent.
Warm fire,
Getting drier,
Money, money spent.

Christmas, Christmas dinner,
Tummy in a spinner.
All full up,
Wine in cup.
Christmas, Christmas dinner.

Jessica Cummins (12)
Parkside Middle School, Bromsgrove

The Autumn Line-Up Has Come

What, that time for coldness!
What, that time for wrapping up!
What, that time for having the fire on!
What, that time for snuggling up!
What, that time, it's autumn again!

Matthew Buckley (13)
Parkside Middle School, Bromsgrove

Troubles Are Like Bubbles

When I've lots of little troubles,
That's the time to watch the bubbles.
Go sailing and sailing to and fro
For the bubbles that I'm making soon will be breaking
And my troubles like the bubble will all go.

Faye Stanley (12)
Parkside Middle School, Bromsgrove

October

The weather of October,
Crispy leaves,
Floating smoothly along
The top of the wind.
Green, yellow and orange trees,
blending together in the deep dark forest.
Hallowe'en with scary masks, ghosts and witches' brooms.
Sweets and treats and tubs full of snacks.
Cold, windy and rainy weather,
Brollies and furry, fluffy coats.
Birthday parties and celebrations
With cakes and candles and yummy chocolate treats.
When October's over, then comes November.

Abbey Brett (13)
Parkside Middle School, Bromsgrove

Reign Of Chaos

In a land of power
Where great warriors dwell
People prepare for war.

For a great threat
Is upon this land
Which will spell the end
For this magic land.

Only the most ruthless
Will survive.
Only the strongest
Will survive this
Reign of chaos.

Daniel Hemming (12)
Parkside Middle School, Bromsgrove

Playground

Silence as lessons run,
So quiet as people stare out of the window.
Children wondering how long,
How long until they run around
Can't wait until they snack.

Yelling as children play,
Noise as adults watch.
Teachers in the playground wondering how long.
How long until they stop making noise
Can't wait until the snack ends.

Time has ended how long until the next
Wishing it never ends.
Time has ended how long to another
Wishing it never started
But it starts all over again.

Tom Melbourne (12)
Parkside Middle School, Bromsgrove

I Look Out My Window And See . . .

I look out my window and see,
blue sky and clouds that are white
and a black and yellow busy bee,
a man flying his blue and red kite.

I look out my window and hear,
a car speeding past,
a bus coming near,
a bike riding fast.

I look out my window and count
how many cars go by,
red, blue, yellow, black
and I see a plane fly,
a man giving his dog a smack.

I look out my window and see people play,
a woman mowing her lawn
and watching the time go by day by day
and I see a baby yawn.

Phil Southall (13)
Parkside Middle School, Bromsgrove

Me!

Sometimes my life feels empty,
Sometimes my life feels full,
Sometimes I think I can do anything,
Sometimes I think I can do nothing.

Sometimes I feel happy,
Sometimes I feel sad,
Sometimes I feel jealous,
Sometimes I feel energetic.

Sometimes I feel I want to boom,
Sometimes sleep sounds special,
Sometimes friends make me over the moon,
Sometimes I feel small.

Sometimes friends are what everyone needs,
Sometimes that is the best,
Sometimes I'm so lucky,
Because I've got plenty!

Emily Claydon (12)
Parkside Middle School, Bromsgrove

Fly By

Just like a bird, I fly by,
Just like a bird, I fly high,
Time seems to rush by me so, so fast,
Ten minutes ago seems like the past.

Whoosh! goes the wind, down the street,
Watch the people lift their feet,
Feeling happy as they walk right by,
Looking up at the big, bright blue sky.

Just like a bird, I fly by,
Just like a bird, I fly high,
As the raindrops prance on the ground,
The children from the streets dance around.

Laura Baxter (12)
Parkside Middle School, Bromsgrove

The Waiting Man

There he was, stood all alone,
cold or hot, he was stood like stone,
he's waiting for her,
maybe, just maybe, he should go back home.

She divorced him years ago
and said, 'I'll come back,'
things were rotten for him,
he even got the sack.

His feet felt like they were holding weights,
flies all over him, gosh he was in a terrible state,
he was seeing tall trees, thought it was her,
so he looked even harder and it turned into a blur.

Now it reached winter, here comes the snow,
did not stop looking the way she went
did not have time to set up a tent
maybe he should let this one go.

Daniel Crane (13)
Parkside Middle School, Bromsgrove

Five Companions

Five companions travelling west,
From their own home,
On a mission that is not known,
The only thing they know is:
'Keep to the west until
You reach the red bridge'.

Their homes are so far away,
So, so far away.
The companions, if you saw them,
Would look rather strange,
Two women, three men,
All dressed ready for war.
Except one woman in a dress
Of green and blue.

They have many, many enemies,
In the north.
They know nothing yet,
But they will soon find out,
Where it is they are to go.

Far, far into the west and north,
Until they come to the ruby red bridge.
The sun shines down like a smile,
The moon shines down like a sleeping baby.

They travelled far up
The weird, whirling, wonderful road.
The road was like a snake,
A black snake with leaves
And conkers all over.

Many people looked at them,
For in the year 2000 BC,
It was strange to see them.
One day they will reach the bridge
And find their mission.

Casey Nokes (13)
Parkside Middle School, Bromsgrove

School, Oh, School

School, school is not cool,
It's not even worth your drawl,
If you think it is, you're a fool,
The best thing is dribbling
With a football.

The teachers look so fair and calm,
But really at break they're licking on a lip balm,
When they hear the morning alarm,
They think, *oh no, I've got to go*
Into those barmy lot at the farm.

At the end of the day,
You hope it's soon May,
For it's your holiday,
But then you forget,
It's detention to pay.

Emma Broom (12)
Parkside Middle School, Bromsgrove

A Bug's Party

The bug party was loud and banging
With lots of noise and chilling
The music was pop
The costumes were hip
A bug's party of the year
There was lots of singing
Lots of eating
Everybody came as spiders
And creepy-crawlies
A bug's party of the year.

Kelly Davitt (12)
Parkside Middle School, Bromsgrove

School Life

I don't like English,
I don't like maths,
I don't like sitting,
In the old school class.

I don't like history,
I don't like French,
I don't like sitting,
On the cold, school bench.

I like it when it's break time,
I like it when it's lunch,
I like it when it's home time,
When someone throws a punch.

Amy Youster (12)
Parkside Middle School, Bromsgrove

The Night Girl

The night girl in the star
Is looking at me from afar,
Watch her gracefully fly
Through the midnight sky.

Look! she's over there,
Behind her flows her long hair,
Down her face trickles a tear,
She looks afraid, full of fear.

She wears a silky, long dress,
She looks like she's trying to impress,
Has she ever been in love?
As she watches me from above.

It's like she reaches out and touches me,
Who's making her sad, can't they just let her be?
What on earth has she done?
The graceful flight turns to a run.

She screams a weeping cry,
What is going on, is she going to die?
I can't see nor hear her anymore,
I can now see a light through a door.

I now know that scared girl was me,
But now my innerside has been set free,
I'm now dancing in the sky,
Now the broken wing is fixed, I'm able to fly.

Laura Halfpenny (13)
Parkside Middle School, Bromsgrove

Spider

Spider slid slowly
Down a piece of web
And landed on a piece of lead.

Silly spider didn't know
That he could die
If he said bye-bye.

Spider had the lead for tea
And with a smile that's wide
Lay down and sighed.

Little spider died in peace
And a good turnout came
To his final lane.

Sophie Hazell (12)
Parkside Middle School, Bromsgrove

My Poem On Sport

I like sport, it is cool!
You can swim a race in the pool.
You can jump the hurdles on the track,
Or you can hit the ball with a whack.

I like sport, it is cool!
You can play sport at school.
Or you can throw the ball in the hoop.
You can score a goal with a loop.

I like sport, it is cool!
You can be a judge on the stool.
You can watch the race from the start
And watch the runners taking part.

I like sport, it is cool!
Watch me make a fool.
That's my poem about sport.
That is the lesson I am taught.

Kate Walters (12)
Parkside Middle School, Bromsgrove

Wondering

Have you thought about when you die?
Do you go up to the place in the sky?
Will you fall down below?
Keep on thinking because you will never know.
Will you go to Heaven or will you go to Hell,
Or will the spirits take you as you yell?
How do they decide whether you go up or down?
Will you be a slave or will you wear the crown?
When will it be your time to go?
Keep on dreaming because you will never know.

Owen Long (12)
Parkside Middle School, Bromsgrove

The Village

In the snow, black and green,
Why no white? You may ask,
Maybe the people like the mess?

I think this mess didn't come naturally,
Standing high in the sky, the old factory's working,
All the waste coming out, like a toilet tube.

But could these things cause this mess?
Still, I think another reason may be,
The village is cursed, an ancient one at that.

This place would seem horrible to me and you,
But they look like they enjoy it.
Why no effort to clear it up? There must be a reason.

If I could go out there,
Instead of being locked up here, ha, ha, ha,
Ha, ha, ha, ha, I would show them a mess, ha!

Sam Morris (12)
Parkside Middle School, Bromsgrove

My Bad Dream

In the night,
I'd bolt up and scream,
I'd call for my mom,
As I'd had a bad dream.

I'd sit up in bed,
I'd sweat and worry,
Out of her room,
My mom would hurry.

I'd settle back down,
Try and get to sleep,
All of my duvet,
Would be in a heap.

I wouldn't stop thinking,
About this dream,
My ears would be ringing
With the sound of a scream.

About an hour later,
I'd settle to sleep,
I'd have a happy dream,
Something like sheep.

No more worrying,
No more screams,
That is the poem,
Of my bad dreams.

Danielle Hill (12)
Parkside Middle School, Bromsgrove

Fish

We went to the garden centre,
To buy a little, baby fish.
I picked one, the funny one,
So we put him in the bag.

And took him back to my house,
I was so excited too.
To put him in the round, plastic bowl,
I dropped him on the kitchen floor.

He was like a jumping, jolly, jelly,
On the marble floor, but,
Now the poor little fish is down in the dump,
He had such a short life.

Sophie Tilley (13)
Parkside Middle School, Bromsgrove

Girl In The Park!

I see it every day,
When I am in the park,
It sits down under a tree,
All alone in the dark.

I wonder what it is,
Sat all alone over there,
It looks so sad, lonely, cold,
With its long, flowing hair.

As the night goes by,
I begin to fall asleep,
But then I am woken up,
By a loud and scared weep.

I look straight over at the tree,
The one that it was by,
Nothing was in my sight,
But behind a bench, I hear a cry.

I then look behind the bench,
To see what is there,
I see a young girl,
As I begin to stare.

She looks so sad, lonely, cold,
Sat there all alone,
I wonder if she has a friend,
Or maybe even a home?

No one cares about this girl,
No one cares she's here,
Now she knows she's got a friend
And that someone is near.

Lucy Howard (12)
Parkside Middle School, Bromsgrove

Confused I Am

I am
a gong,
that gets rattled and battled,
a toy,
lost in the darkness of the wood,
a bird,
that squeaks instead of sings,
the friend that doesn't mend.

I am
the world spinning round and round,
the wheels on a bike being worn away and rusty,
a leaf,
that doesn't stop spinning,
the clock spinning that no one can stop.

I am
a paintbrush with no bristles,
a book that is read back to front,
a snail,
with swirls that look like a pale pink pearl,
an alien on an unknown planet.

I am
a frost that is dew in summer,
the sun in a raincoat and hat,
a raindrop that is hit with a bat,
the stolen spring that I named as a ring.

Hannah Walker (12)
St Bede's Catholic Middle School, Redditch

My Dream

Once upon a time, a girl lay in bed,
With thoughts in her head.
She dreamt of the monkeys or gorillas you might say,
She wanted to sleep,
They wanted to play.
She tried to run,
She tried to hide,
'Leave me alone!' she cried and cried.
But the gorillas never gave in,
They had two little hairs on their chinny chin chins.
They chased and chased,
Made it into a race,
Then *stop!*

All of a sudden,
The girl could hide no more,
She lay there, still and alone on the floor.
They had worn her out,
Frightened her no doubt.
She looked up,
'Oh you mucky pup!'
It was Mum and Dad,
Not looking mad,
There she saw two big grins
And two little hairs on their chinny chin chins.

Katy McCullagh (11)
St Bede's Catholic Middle School, Redditch

I Am Frustrated

I am
The mouse
Forever avoiding the trap
The runner
That never ends the long and looping lap
The student
That looks at the empty answer gap.

I am
The chewing gum
That sticks to every shopper's shoe
The naughty boy
Whose work will never do
The safari animals
Stuck in the zoo.

I am
The parting
Which never is straight
The woman
That can't ever lose weight
The man
Who never gets a date.

I am
The mum
Who can't remove the stain
The horse
That has a knotted mane
The batty old woman
Who *does* have a brain.

Frustration is surely the worst emotion;
Please, someone, give me the healing potion.

Amber O'Shaughnessy (12)
St Bede's Catholic Middle School, Redditch

Sunset

The day is ending,
On high, the sky is burning.
The colours splay,
The colours merge,
Purples, reds and oranges.

A bloody gash,
Slashes through the heavens.
All creatures lay down their heads
And bow down to their fiery lord.

The whole Earth,
Gives praise to the king of day.
The lord of light,
Pays homage to the queen of night,
The lady of dark.

As the sun,
Sinks through the ground
And the birds serenade the dying day,
There is a splendour of light and sound.

James Murphy (11)
St Bede's Catholic Middle School, Redditch

I Am A River

I am a waterfall, crashing heavily on the big boulders and rough rocks,
Water that ends in a plunge pool and ends near the sea by the docks,
I start as a river meandering through the flood plains,
Forming and making land, rocks I gain,
Never have time to stop and think,
I am like a giant sink.

I am a waterfall, a cascade of water,
Reforming land, rocks and sand I slaughter,
Eroding the bottom,
Making it rotten,
But still the river continues.

I am a river,
Flowing as fast as I can,
Participating in a running race, don't even need a fan,
No time to breathe, no time to stop,
No time to skip, no time to hop,
Smashing up the hard rock,
Softening the soft rock,
Making a drop of hundreds of metres,
We, waterfalls, are like hungry eaters.

I am a river,
Reaching a bend,
A meander, it's called as I come near an end,
I come out of my box and stretch my body wide,
As I come to the sea crashing the side,
I see young children playing in the soft, golden sand,
I see adults trying to wash their hands,
On my weightless stomach, they swim,
They start to go home as the sun goes dim,
I'll carry on tomorrow and see what it brings,
I am a river, full of wonderful things.

Natasha Daplyn (13)
St Bede's Catholic Middle School, Redditch

Tutan-Tutak-Tiffed

Scientists were baffled,
Geniuses were miffed,
When they heard of the unchartered island,
Tutan-Tutak-Tiffed.

They set out in their wollycopter,
To explore the unexplored,
When they set down on anticipated ground,
They were amazed by what they saw:

A hundred bulbous, blunkerput bushes,
A thousand quarrelling quarms,
One or two ostrirhinogoats
And a cat and dog with horns.

A gaseous, glooping globbertoad,
A bird that shot nuts from its beak,
Some grass that bit you if you stepped on it
And a plant that engulfed you with a squeak.

The scientists and geniuses jumped into their wollycopter
And from the ground they did lift.
So shocked were they, that they vowed that day,
Never to return to the island of
Tutan-Tutak-Tiffed.

James Down (11)
St Bede's Catholic Middle School, Redditch

The Rainbow

Red is the fire that keeps everybody warm
on a cold winter's day.

Orange is a juicy, ripening fruit
ready to be picked.

Yellow is the hot, gleaming sun
shining all the time.

Green is the soft, freshly cut grass
blowing in the springtime breeze.

Blue is an ocean, long and ongoing
and no one can see the end.

Indigo is the sky, just before it gets dark
and turns black.

Violet is a pretty flower that blooms
only in the summer.

Grace Taylor & Maria Hore (11)
St Bede's Catholic Middle School, Redditch

Predator And Prey

The cheetah waits,
The deer bounds,
The cheetah waits,
The deer is found.

The cheetah pounces
Off his feet,
The helpless deer,
Dodging and dipping.

Finally, the two actually meet,
The cheetah's claws,
Gripping and ripping.

The prey is down,
The predator is king,
The dead deer is meatless now,
The smell rises and the vultures sing . . .

James Brandon (12)
St Bede's Catholic Middle School, Redditch

I Am A Waterfall

I am the mind of the waterfall, controlling every beat, move and race,
I am the heart of the waterfall, controlling every pulse
That runs through my body.
I am the head of the waterfall, looking down on the steep rock face,
Preparing to fall.

I am the body of the waterfall, mean and lean, long and strong,
I am the leg of the waterfall, running smoothly
And then pacing myself swiftly.
I am the drop of the waterfall, the moment's getting tense,
I am the power of the waterfall, I could knock down a fence.

I am the emotion of the waterfall, anger, happiness and sadness,
I'm all alone in this place called the world,
When people come to see my gracefulness,
I am a story that has been told.

In the cold, winter months when I am frozen,
There is nothing left to see.
I am still visited by people,
Why can't they just let me be?

Lauren O'Brien (12)
St Bede's Catholic Middle School, Redditch

Happy I Am

I am
The shiny
New book that everyone wants to read
The piece
Of good advice that everyone seems to need
The brand new trainers that everyone wants
The new computer with all the new fonts
The beautiful, exotic garden that you wish to see
The door that has a shiny, new key.

I am
The laughter
Of his friends
The happiness
With no end
The new computer game that you want to play
The post that comes every day
The flower poking through the weeds
The flower growing from new garden seeds.

David Phelan (12)
St Bede's Catholic Middle School, Redditch

Sad I Am

I am,
The heart,
That's lost its beat,
The lungs
That will no longer pump oxygen through the body,
The corpse,
That has no soul to bare.

I am,
The person,
Who wants somebody to care for,
The nobody,
Who's left behind a closed door,
The mother,
With no child,
The dog,
With no owner.

I am,
The remote,
With no batteries,
The siren,
With no voice,
The puzzle,
With no pieces.

I am,
The stocking,
With no presents in it,
The rod,
With no bait,
The witch,
With no wand.

I am the girl who is depressed and forgotten.

Annabell McAuliffe (12)
St Bede's Catholic Middle School, Redditch

Help

As I was walking down the lane,
I saw them dripping in the rain,
They were waiting for me, I knew,
Bob, John, Sam, Claire and Sue,
I wanted to run,
I wanted to hide,
But if I did they would think I lied,
I promised them I would,
They said that I should,
I worked all day and night too,
I was sick and worn down,
So I started to frown,
I didn't like being bullied,
It wasn't very nice,
I was rolled about, I felt like a dice,
I wanted it to stop,
I wanted to shout,
Help!

Laura Cunning (11)
St Bede's Catholic Middle School, Redditch

I Am Poem

I am
    a cat
        running from a dog,
    a car
        that's lost in fog,
    a hedgehog
        in the road,
    a labourer
        scared of dropping a heavy load.

I am
    a whale
        stranded in the ocean,
    a witch
        without a potion,
    a baby
        that's lost its cry,
    a man
        that is very shy.

I am
    a dog
        that's lost its bark,
    the big, blue sea
        with a great white shark,
    a rabbit
        with one eye,
    a goblin
        called Sly.

I am
    a door
        without a key,
    a girl that cannot see,
    a calendar
        with no dates,
    a lonely girl
        without any mates.

Jordan-Leigh Norman (12)
St Bede's Catholic Middle School, Redditch

Depression

I am
The triggeration
Which sets off decontamination,
The man shot and killed
Before he had happiness fulfilled,
The bullied, little child
With stones hitting him at wild.

I am
The small figure of a soldier
Being replaced by a folder,
The broken toy car
Which has been trampled on, then thrown really far,
The sock which should be clean
But has gone a mouldy green.

I am
The dirty wrecked car
Choking on tar,
The doll with no head,
The troll without friends, nor a bed,
The carpet left alone and has now filled with vomit,
The crying cartoon man, who accidentally killed Gromit.

I am
The book that shall never be opened
Just because of its cover,
The claustrophobic kid,
Crushed head-first in his own crib,
The anger of the beast
Trying not to be released.

I am
Trapped in a prison
For something I didn't do,
Inside some sort of nut
Running out of air and sucking in my gut.

I am
Carrying the burden of Hell.

Christy Connolly (12)
St Bede's Catholic Middle School, Redditch

Happy I Am

I am
The brightest poppy in the poppy field.
The bright-coloured flower in the bouquet.
The new, sparkling water that everyone wants a taste of.
The reddest rose on the bush.

I am
The sun on the hottest day of the year.
The scorching sun that powers the Earth.
The sunny day that no one wants to waste.
The planet that everyone wants to live on.
The flame that heats your home.
The mug of hot chocolate on a cold winter's night.

I am
The new, shiny ring on a newly wedded bride.
The book that everyone wants to read.
As happy as a girl with a new teddy.
A hug from a close friend.
As happy as a newborn baby.

Stephanie Taylor
St Bede's Catholic Middle School, Redditch

Successful I Am

I am
The cherry
On the grand cake
The winner
Who breaks the tape at the finish line
The conker
Which won every battle.

I am
The weakest bird
That can fly the highest
The shyest magician
That can perform the best show
The most confused child
Which can produce the best work.

I am
The tallest sunflower
From which the smallest seed grew
The strongest elephant
Which was once the weakling
The most fierce lion
Which was known to be the most scared.

I am the star that is noticed from everywhere
I am the bestseller which is known by everyone
I am the horse that won everyone's bet.

I am the most successful of them all.

Rachel White (12)
St Bede's Catholic Middle School, Redditch

Mixed Feelings I Am

I am
A new flower
Just picked for your mom
The garden
On which the sun has shone
A daffodil
Bright and yellow
The poppy
That is never mellow.

I am
A light
With no shine left
The room
That is always a mess
A little girl
That God will not bless
The only fish
That swims in Loch Ness.

I am
The smell
Of Christmas dinner
The taste
Of being a winner

Fahren Lee (12)
St Bede's Catholic Middle School, Redditch

Sad I Am

I am
The wind that nobody listens to.
The punchbag that everyone takes a piece out of.
The man that everyone ignores.

I am
The rainy day that everyone hated.
The cloudy sky that blocks the sun.
The sun that hasn't learnt to rise.

I am
The smashed window that no one has replaced.
The house that nobody lives in.
The derelict factory that hasn't been used for years.

I am
The car that has been dumped on the side of the road.
The train that has been sent to the scrapyard.
The lorry that hasn't delivered anything for centuries.

Liam Scriven (12)
St Bede's Catholic Middle School, Redditch

Happy I Am

I am
The garden
Full of wonderful flowers.
The butterfly
Fluttering into the sun.
The kitten
Playing with a ball of wool.

I am
The smell
Of a bacon sandwich on a Sunday morning.
The scent
Of incense candles burning away.
The whiff
Of chicken cooking in an oven.
The bouncy ball
Full of bounce.

I am
The smell
Of chocolate at Cadbury World.
The big bag of sweets
Bursting in the air.
The pot of gold
At the end of a rainbow.
The battery full of energy.

I am
The cheering
Of a winning team.
The bright sun
On a rainy day.
The library book
Full of colour.
The torch
That shows the way in the dark.

Cassandra Bate-Jones (12)
St Bede's Catholic Middle School, Redditch

In My Head

In my head there's nothing at all
Except a railway
Every hour there's a train
Which drops off a peanut brain.

As well as a brain
There's a nagging old mum
Who nags me to clean my room.

My room is such a mess
Because I've got a small brain
So I don't tidy it
Because I've got a peanut brain.

I know a brain reader
I told him about my peanut brain
But he didn't believe me
So I told him again.

Now I say bye-bye
Because I don't know what to say
Except all the brainless people out there
Look after your peanut brain.

Harry Meads (12)
St Bede's Catholic Middle School, Redditch

Doze Close Sleepy Goes

Doze, close sleepy goes into the world of nightmares.

As I drift up the short, green lawn,
To the tree which seems to have a brown bark door.

I enter the trunk of the tree . . .
Then all of a sudden there are spiders crawling all over me.

I run from the tree as my energy starts to lack
And then I see there's a humongous spider upon my back.

As I roll on the grass
I feel my phobia of spiders is let loose.

I slowly wake out of the world of nightmares,
Light appears,
As my mind clears,
Awake and the fear disappears.

Jodie Ollis (11)
St Bede's Catholic Middle School, Redditch

I Am

I am the bird
singing happily
in the tree,
the tune that
the bird sings.

I am the chewing gum
that never ever
loses its taste,
the chocolate that
everyone wants to taste.

I am a garden
filled with bright yellow
and red flowers,
the storybook that everyone
wants to read.

I am the yellow sun
driving away the storm,
the toothpaste
which cleans your teeth.

I am the clay
that shapes the hand,
the river growing
into a lake.

I am a boy playing happily
in the shade,
the wave that
halts the sea.

I am an antique ring
that everyone cherishes,
the water that will
quench your thirst.

I am the green grass
that grows on the land,
the tree growing
big and strong.

I am the cat
eating the rat for dinner,
the waterfall eroding
the rock away.

Ali Khan (12)
St Bede's Catholic Middle School, Redditch

Happy I Am

I am
Fire full of light and spark
That light that helps you in the dark.

I am
The fresh smell of home-made bread
And the look of a newly wed.

I am
Treated like a king
And the shine in a diamond ring.

I am
The bird with the sweetest *tweet tweet*
The runner with the fastest feet.

I am
The firefly full of glow
The clothes shop's prettiest, shiny bow.

I am
The best dinner dress
Your beautiful face without the stress.

I am
A lively train full of steam
A sparkling shoe full of gleam.

I am
Happy
Yes I am.

Martyn Cooke & Charlie Rowe (12)
St Bede's Catholic Middle School, Redditch

I'm Late

I'm late
I'm late
I'm late
I'm late
I'm late

The birds sing
Far away the bell rings
Mum shouts
Gotta get out
Clothes on
Breakfast gone
Out the door
I fall on the floor
On I run, this isn't fun
Gotta get to school
But I'm outta fuel
I got to the playground
Then I look all around
Then I run inside
There's the teacher, I can't hide
Then she says . . .

You're late
You're late
You're very, very late!

Emily Heaven (11)
St Bede's Catholic Middle School, Redditch

A New Family Member

For as long as I can remember,
I've wanted a cat,
But Dad wasn't keen,
So that, I was told, was that.

Many years later,
On an ordinary day,
I was sent, after school,
Round a friend's house, to play.

Mom and Dad had
An errand to run,
'Won't be long!' they said,
'We'll soon be done!'

I arrived home
And walked through the door,
I saw a pet carrier,
Positioned on the floor.

I stared real hard,
Not knowing what to think,
Then two, bright eyes,
Began to blink.

'Who's this?' I exclaimed,
Not believing what I saw,
Just as the kitten,
Offered a tiny, black paw.

He's yours if you'd like him,
He's in need of a name,
I expect he's getting hungry,
If not, try a game.

That was three years ago,
It seems like no time,
Dad is real keen now,
Him and Todd get on fine!

Hannah Louise Delli-Bovi (11)
St Bede's Catholic Middle School, Redditch

Roller Coaster I Am

I am
The bunny
Bonny and gay
The shining sun's
Dazzling ray
I am the excitement of Christmas Day.

I am
The sky
Clear and blue
The baby's blanket
Crisp and new
I am the tiger escaping the zoo.

But now the door is firmly closed
And I am now left all alone
My heart lets out a silent groan.

I am
The boots
Dusty and worn
The old shirt
Faded and torn
I am the flakes without the corn.

I am
The crumpled paper thrown aside
The heartbroken lady
Never a bride
I am the failure stripped of pride.

I used to be the delicate lace,
The china doll, fair of face,
But now I'm forgotten, not a trace.

Clare Williams (13)
St Bede's Catholic Middle School, Redditch

Happy I Am

I am
The letter
That I remembered to send
A friend's problem
That I can mend
A hug
From a closest friend.

I am
The best flower
In a bride's bouquet
The winning team
In croquet
The best game
That everybody wants to play.

I am
A healthy
Little buzzing bee
The brightest light
On a Christmas tree
The cleanest
Sparkling, colourful sea.

I am
The battery
That has just been charged
The poem
That has been enlarged.

I am
The joy of children
On Christmas Day
The happy horse's
Jolly neigh
The rabbit
That has got his hay.

I am
The flame
Which warms your room
The most expensive
Decorative plume
The happiest
Smartest, wedding day groom.

Gemma Giordan (12)
St Bede's Catholic Middle School, Redditch

Guilty I Am

I am
The glossy model
Two-timing rich people with lots of mates
The pickpocketer
Who robbed Bill Gates
Holding the Queen hostage
In her room, at her palace.

I am
The smuggler
Who smuggled an illegal immigrant
The man
Who committed accidental murder
Shoplifting
An army-based grenade launcher.

I am
The Statue of Liberty on fire from a match
Calling my friend a dog with a catch
Assaulting a police officer without a thought
The naughty woman lying in court.

I am
The boy
Playing ball and breaking Mom's £1,000,000 vase
The hijacker
Who stopped the flight to Mars
The surgeon
With a fake diploma.

Jonathan Evans (12)
St Bede's Catholic Middle School, Redditch

Belgium

Just its flat and smooth countryside,
As the sea bides its tide,
Lots of people fly their kites
And some prefer to see the sights.

Some go to the beach
And some like to teach,
Some go to college,
To scratch up on their knowledge.

It's slow, but nice in lots of ways,
So some stay for a couple of days,
Take it easy, take a rest
And its chocolates are definitely the best!

Kathryn Martin (11)
St Mary's RC High School, Hereford

The Winds Of Change

The nights draw in, the feeling's cold,
The sun goes down, the wind is bold.
The leaves they fly up in the sky,
And on the ground they fall and die.

In desperation everything flees,
As bareness falls upon the trees.
Animals start to hibernate,
As the rest of us stay here and wait.

Plants and animals have to cope,
The only thing now to do, is hope.
While ducks and birds all fly south,
Everything falls into winter's mouth.

Autumn has gone and winter's here,
The frost so cold it brings a tear.
The hats and scarves, they all come out,
At each new day we hurry about.

Each morning comes, the curtains drawn,
Peeping out to see what's on the lawn.
Then one day there comes a call,
From white skies does the snow downfall.

A smile appears, we all rush out,
Shrieks of joy are all about.
The snow, we roll up in a ball,
While others hide behind the wall.

As fun and laughter's all around,
The snow stops falling on the ground.
The sledges stop, put away the gear,
The winter starts to disappear.

The winds they warm, the sun arrives,
The bees, they buzz up in their hives.
The birds fly home to build a nest,
For new young ones, they want the best.

The sound of spring shrills through the trees,
The fragrance fresh amongst the breeze.
The ground opens up and buds appear,
A sure sign that spring is here.

Julianne Clark (11)
St Mary's RC High School, Hereford

Storms

Tiny droplets of water,
Bounce up and down on umbrellas,
While thunder crashes
And lightning flashes.
The cold wind howls
And blows everything around,
People run for shelter,
While sharp rain falls on their heads.
Torrents of water flow,
On the edge of slippery roads,
Windscreen wipers waving madly,
But still the windows are blurred,
Watching puddles form.
Everyone at home is cold,
With blankets wrapped around them.
Grey skies come,
With big, dark clouds,
Now hail starts,
Hard and bitter.

Amy Flynn (11)
St Mary's RC High School, Hereford

People

There is no such thing as two people alike
Everybody's different, never the same,
Whether black, white or yellow, we belong to the human race,
Sometimes we tease others because they look different,
We make them feel down, like they don't belong,
But how would we feel if we had to move country,
Away from family and friends
And to make things worse, we were being bullied because we look
different?

Think before acting, that's my message.

Laura Jones (11)
St Mary's RC High School, Hereford

Charge Of The Orchestra

(Based on 'Charge of the Light Brigade' by Alfred Lord Tennyson)

Half a note, half a note,
Half a note onward.
Into the valley of silence,
Played the six hundred.
First came the string section,
With a pluck, scrape and bow.
Next was the brass, with a mighty blow,
Thirdly the woodwind, dancing as they go.

Forte the orchestra braved the percussion,
As brass stampeded along,
Woodwind burst into song,
Music echoed round and round,
Causing the most elegant sound,
Bursting into silence valley, with a bound.

Silence to the right of them,
Silence to the left of them,
Silence in front of them,
But they carried on,
Boldly they played and well,
Silence was banished! A story to tell,
Played the six hundred.

Eva Howard (11)
St Mary's RC High School, Hereford

The Four Seasons

First comes spring,
When many rabbits play.
Next comes summer,
When the sun shines all day.
The autumn comes,
When leaves are falling.
And last comes winter,
When the cold winds are calling.
This jumble of months are important to hear,
Because these four seasons,
Make up a whole year!

Mollie-Rose Russell (11)
St Mary's RC High School, Hereford

The Tree

The tree was a wrinkled hand,
Old and young.
It flexes its young fingers
And creaks its old bones.
It whispers secrets all day
And is a friend, in a way.

It waves to you,
It sings to me
And flakes off its brownish skin.
Its green fingernails brush your hair,
Or creep around you and draw you in.
It beckons,
It dances,
It sings and calls to you.

Glittering jewellery,
Or ripe, shiny fruit,
Hang from its laden boughs.
It breathes out,
Sighs gently,
Whilst whispering a song:
'Forever old, yet always young . . .
The tree.'

Emily Lunn (11)
St Mary's RC High School, Hereford

The Path Of Life

Over acres it may seem
But may the sun so beam,
When you reach your goal
Where many bells do toll
And though caution on the path you seek
You shall meet a boy both lowly and meek.
He will tell you which road to take
Where seabirds screech and the waves break.
But on your feet you must stay,
For then comes a man who will take you away.
Many are the dangers with which your path is fraught
And many a death has it sought,
But if you get that far anyway
And live to see the break of day,
Your glory shall be rich and deep
And for evermore you can keep,
When you reach your goal,
Where many bells do toll.

Josie Walters (11)
St Mary's RC High School, Hereford

Life!

Size 8, size 10, size 12,
What a dilemma!
Red, pink or blue,
What a dilemma!
Button, zip or ribbon,
What a dilemma!
Patterned, plain or stripes,
What a dilemma!
Buying my clothes,
Such a dilemma!

Size 3, size 4, size 5,
What a nightmare!
Black, blue or brown,
What a nightmare!
Buckle, lace or Velcro,
What a nightmare!
Shoe, boot or sandal,
What a nightmare!
Buying my shoes,
Such a nightmare!

Clothes, shoes and make-up,
Oh, what a choice!
Cinema, bowling or disco,
Oh, what a choice!
Friends, family or boyfriends,
Oh, what a choice!
Life,
Full of decisions!

Hannah Wilkins (13)
Tenbury High School, Tenbury Wells

Please Listen To Me

I am a teddy bear and I'm here for you
To listen and laugh and to comfort you.
My eyes glisten and I always smile
I just wish you'd listen to me for a while.
Behind my bright eyes, the sadness I hide
Feelings suppressed deep down inside.
Through it all I listen and advise.
When you are sad, through it you rise.
I'm here if you need a shoulder to cry on
I'm a reliable friend who you can count on.
But when you are through it and happy again
Do you see what becomes of your faithful friend?
I am just left there to gather the dust.
Your silence, to me, it is not just.
For I am lonely, quiet and sad
Thinking of all the sad times I've had.
I just wait to be picked up by you again
When you need me to be your friend.
But just for once won't you listen to me
And return the favour? But you don't see.
I have lived a life of gloom
But I would like a teddy soon.
A teddy that I would not forget
I wouldn't leave it alone, not yet.
For teddies are useful - we all have one
But for a sad case, mine I'd pass on
So the world could be happy and sadness free
But for once, could you stop and listen to me?

Louise Nugent (15)
The Dyson Perrins CE High School, Malvern

Crystallised Rose

So pretty yet so still,
So fragile yet unbreakable,
His gradual dying,
Only hearing the rain crying.

Looks indestructible,
But with one touch all is destroyed,
His head falling apart,
The colour getting slowly drained out.

His beauty preserved with armour,
A defeat looks impossible.
But under the covering is just a fragile boy,
Who wants the sun to let him grow again.

But if the sun rises, will he just melt?
Once being picked there's no going back.
There will never be more movement,
Sadness ensures this.

I look at that boy
Then think, there he goes,
Like a crystallised rose.

Katy Warran
The Dyson Perrins CE High School, Malvern

Who Are Those People?

'Who are those people
Up there in the sky?
How do they get there
And how do they fly?'
This child can see,
See far beyond the clouds,
See the beautiful people,
With white wings and white shrouds.
'I know these people,
I've seen them before.
They've been in my sleep,
In my dreams galore.'
And know who they are,
They're seen at night.
Each face a star.
'They are watching us,
Guiding us,
Loving us
And waiting for us . . .'
One day it'll be our turn
To take our souls away.
Then we can watch our loved ones,
Watch them in every way.

Caroline Tandy (14)
The Dyson Perrins CE High School, Malvern

Untitled

Sitting alone in the dark of night
One bright and splendid day,
My eyes focused on a piece of paper
Not knowing what to say.
I wanted to pour my heart out
Let the pain bleed through my pen,
But the words were stifled,
No thoughts came from within.
It's then I realised
My heart was bare black.
No words to say or tears to cry,
Nothing left to attack.
What can I write about nothing,
Except it's pure and vast
Like an empty valley on winter's eve
Here lies my soul, darkened by the past.
This feeling is all I know
Similar to groping in the dark.
I only see this pain I feel
Along with its ancient mark.
It's only now I see my true self
For what am I?
Just an empty, hollow creature.
So I'll curl up with my word
And cry upon my ink,
For every time I write now
I can feel my heart sink.

Laura Sefton (16)
The Dyson Perrins CE High School, Malvern

The Sea

The sea is a hungry lion,
Enormous and dark.
He hunts on the beach all day
With his clashing teeth and shaggy jaws.
He jumps onto his prey
And rips them to bits,
Creeping, crashing against the wall.

Kirsty Jones
The Dyson Perrins CE High School, Malvern

You

You are my life, my heart, my soul.
You are the reason I live in this wretched world.
This world in which people are killing, suffering.
But you, you save me, you give me shelter.
You wrap your arms around me and the storm ceases.
Silence, and all I see is you.
And then, you smile,
A smile that speaks the truth, the mind.
The smile of an angel,
The smile of an angel in love.
A love that is true and deep.
Like the ocean, pure and everlasting.
A love to die for.
A love that I cannot live without.
You close your eyes and you are swallowed up in a deep passion.
Passion that burns like an eternal fire, ever growing.
And then, a kiss.
A kiss that makes me feel alive.
A kiss that makes the world and life seem unimportant,
Like a pebble in a stream, that passes unnoticed.

Toby Proctor (12)
The Dyson Perrins CE High School, Malvern

Untitled

Alone it is dangerous, with others more so.
Alone it seeks materials, with humans it seeks trust.
Foolish ones' trust helps to sow deceit
While one's absence spawns lies and friends' disagreements.

While at work it is quiet and good,
But its mind is always thinking of ways to betray.
When pay comes, words are its fuel,
To expand on the payment it will receive.
Nothing is done without payment.

It can get itself out of most situations,
Though there is no need to most of the time,
For the minds of men think only short distances ahead
While its mind searches out for things to come.

For knowledge is power and it knows that fact well,
That is why most never hear the truth.
It can trust no one, can tell nothing true.
That is why most will never know it fully.

When the day is over and it is time to sleep,
Its mind awakens from its day of rest.
New things are thought up,
Things that do not really fit with its personality,
Things that are not what one expects to hear.

Tom McSweeny (15)
The Dyson Perrins CE High School, Malvern

Untitled

You can't tell beauty from a glance,
For true beauty is from the heart,
To find true love you can't say,
That I love to every day.
An honest relationship is worked through thick and thin,
Not after one hurdle chucked into the bin.
If destiny is fate then let it decide,
As lies and deceit can never survive.

Anne-Marie Bartlett (15)
The Dyson Perrins CE High School, Malvern

Untitled

Butterflies, flowers and bumblebees
Birds, feathers and willow trees
Don't last for ever, I'm sure you know,
Just like a friendship, friend or foe?

Cats, dogs and bunny rabbits
All go sometime and die like old habits.
Things get lost and we move on,
Forget just a little, then everything's gone.

Hedgehogs, badgers and field mice
All go to sleep and wake up in a trice,
Often come back after sleeping in winter,
But the cold in the winter can sometimes hinder.

But life sometimes means sacrifice
And death comes with the roll of a dice.
Death is not something to fear,
Because like flowers grow, you'll come back every year.

Rachel Nugent (15)
The Dyson Perrins CE High School, Malvern

Growing Up

Opening my eyes for the first time,
Three years later, learning to climb,
Starting pre-school drawing rabbits,
Getting into every single naughty habit,
Primary school's first day for me,
Wondering what I'm having for tea,
Leaving primary school for high school tomorrow.

Hunting for my hero,
Leaving high school for college
And I know all sorts of knowledge,
Passing A levels, jumping around,
Thinking all the rest will turn out sound,
Onto my career, what a thought,
Oh, I've found a guy to court.

Kirsty Barnett (13)
Wigmore High School, Wigmore

Kingsland

As I scanned the marvellous patchwork of fields before me,
I fell into a wonderful dream.
The wind whistled through the trees,
As the leaves merrily skipped along the path.

Lucy Foreman (11)
Wigmore High School, Wigmore

Elton

A little hamlet set in the heart of the countryside,
Rolling hills with lush green grass and woodlands.
Cattle, sheep, horses all grazing in the lush pastures,
While the church bell echoes around from its churchyard.

Megan Taylor (11)
Wigmore High School, Wigmore

The Breeze Of Winter

The winds howl like a wolf on a cliff edge,
The snow sleeping sweetly on the hedge.
Children playing in so many clothes, they can hardly move,
Sleigh bells ringing on a horse and carriage.
Footprints in the snow, as deep as your hand,
Snowmen standing like a motionless man.
The dark night closes with stars that have been painted on,
The day dawns and the whitest snow disappears,
The breeze of winter has gone.

Emma Morris (13)
Wigmore High School, Wigmore

Running

The hunt is on,
To find the one.
As it may seem,
Who did the thing,
That made us scream,
'I'll get you!'

The chase is on,
To get the one.
Who gave out chase,
Who began the race,
Who turned the pace,
And legged it.

The game is on,
To hunt the one.
Who's running,
Whose legs are numbing,
Whose mind is dumbing,
And who I'll get.

The game is done,
I've almost won.
I'll finish the sport,
Which they have fought,
And they had thought,
They'd won.

'Tag, you're it!'
'Hey, no fair, I tripped!'
'Well come and get me then!'

Chris Kay (13)
Wolverley High School, Kidderminster